Find the Truth!

Everything you are about to read is true *except* for one of the sentences on this page.

Which one is **TRUE**?

T or F   The Statue of Liberty used to be someone's house.

T or F   The statue wears a size 879 shoe.

Find the answers in this book.

Contents

The Statue of Liberty

ELAINE LANDAU

Children's Press®
An Imprint of Scholastic Inc.
New York   Toronto   London   Auckland   Sydney
Mexico City   New Delhi   Hong Kong
Danbury, Connecticut

Content Consultant
David R. Smith, PhD
Academic Adviser and Adjunct Assistant Professor of History
University of Michigan-Ann Arbor

Reading Consultant
Linda Cornwell
Literacy Consultant
Carmel, Indiana

Library of Congress Cataloging-in-Publication Data
Landau, Elaine.
 The Statue of Liberty / by Elaine Landau.
    p. cm.—(A True book)
 Includes bibliographical references and index.
 ISBN-13: 978-0-531-12635-6 (lib. bdg.)   978-0-531-14785-6 (pbk.)
 ISBN-10: 0-531-12635-8 (lib. bdg.)   0-531-14785-1 (pbk.)

 1. Statue of Liberty (New York, N.Y.)—Juvenile literature. 2. Statue of Liberty (New York, N.Y.)—
History—Juvenile literature. 3. New York (N.Y.)—Buildings, structures, etc.—Juvenile literature.
I. Title. II. Series.
 F128.64.L6L363 2007
 974.7'1—dc22   2007004180

6 7 8 9 10 R 17 16 15 14 13 12 11

True! Her sandals are 25 feet long— size 879!

If you travel by boat to New York City, the Statue of Liberty's might be the first face you see.

6

CHAPTER 1

A Special Statue for a Special Place

The United States of America! Over time, people from many lands have been drawn to it. People dreamed of coming to the United States for different reasons. Some even risked their lives to do so.

The statue is taller than 12 elephants!

People have been voting in free elections since the United States was founded. But there was a time when only white males could vote.

Some people came to find religious freedom. In the United States, people were free to worship as they pleased. Others came to the United States to find political freedom. Many countries did not hold elections to choose leaders. In some places, it was illegal to disagree with the government. But Americans had fought for the right to express their opinions, and won.

The Statue of Liberty stands close to New York City on its own island, Liberty Island.

Her index finger is
3 feet 6 inches wide. ➡

Many people thought that anything was possible in the United States. Can you think of a better place for a 151-foot (46-meter) statue that represents **liberty**?

The Statue of Liberty is often called Lady Liberty. She proudly stands on Liberty Island, a small island at the entrance to New York Harbor. Before there were airplanes, most people coming to America came by ship into that harbor. Often these people became the newest **citizens** of the United States.

Lady Lightning

One of the commonly asked questions about the statue is: "Has it ever been struck by lightning?"

The answer is yes. The Statue of Liberty gets struck by lightning more than 100 times each year. Lightning usually strikes the tallest thing around. That makes the tall statue a natural target. Lightning doesn't hurt the statue, however. The electricity travels safely down through her metal skin toward the ground.

Frédéric Auguste Bartholdi created large statues in France before he started work on the Statue of Liberty. He made many small models of Lady Liberty in his studio. It took Bartholdi 16 years to finish building the statue and its pedestal.

CHAPTER 2

The Big Idea

Bartholdi built his first big statue, in France, when he was only 18 years old.

The Statue of Liberty is an important American **symbol**. Yet it wasn't made by Americans. It was a gift from France to honor France's long friendship with the United States. A French **sculptor** named Frédéric Auguste Bartholdi was hired by France to do the job.

Celebrating Freedom

Bartholdi began to design his statue in 1870. He knew that American colonists had successfully fought for freedom from England in the late 1700s. This war was called the **Revolutionary War**. France had supported American soldiers by sending money and supplies. Some French soldiers even fought side by side with colonists on the battlefield.

Bartholdi also knew that the United States would celebrate its 100th birthday in 1876. His statue was to represent the freedom that was possible there. What a great gift for a nation's birthday!

Statue of Liberty Timeline

1776
The American colonies declare independence from England.

1870
Bartholdi begins to design the Statue of Liberty.

The sculptor had another reason for creating a statue that stood for liberty. France's **emperor**, Napoleon III, had just lost power. France was forming a new type of government.

Bartholdi and others wanted real freedom for France. They thought that their government should be more like the U.S. government. Then French people would be able to choose their leaders and have more of a say in how their government was run. They hoped that creating the statue would help the French people understand the value of liberty.

1870
France's last emperor, Napoleon III, falls from power.

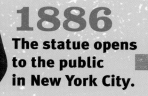

1886
The statue opens to the public in New York City.

The robes

were designed to look like those of a classic Roman goddess.

The poem

at the base of the statue was added in 1903. A poet named Emma Lazarus wrote about the United States taking in people from other countries. This poem has welcomed people from all over the world.

Broken chains

around the statue's feet are a symbol of America's freedom. They also stand for liberty crushing slavery in the United States.

Symbols of Freedom

How many symbols are on Lady Liberty? Take a look. Each part has a different meaning.

The torch

in her right hand lights the path to freedom.

Twenty-five windows

in the crown represent precious stones, gems, and other natural minerals found around the world.

Seven spikes

in the crown stand for Earth's seven seas and seven continents. The oceans are: Arctic, Antarctic, North and South Atlantic, North and South Pacific, and Indian. The continents are: North and South America, Europe, Asia, Africa, Antarctica, and Australia.

The book

in her left hand has the date July 4, 1776, in Roman numerals. That is the date the U.S. Declaration of Independence was adopted.

CHAPTER 3

Making the Dream Come True

Bartholdi was excited about creating a statue that stood for liberty. In 1871, he traveled to the United States. He wanted to get Americans interested in the project. This was important if the Statue of Liberty was ever going to be built.

The statue cost $350,000. Today, that's more than $6 million.

The statue was to be a gift from France. Yet Bartholdi's group could not afford to build it without help. They needed money from Americans.

Even President Ulysses S. Grant met with Bartholdi about the statue.

Bartholdi met with some famous American artists, writers, and businessmen. People seemed to like his ideas. However, no one was ready to give Bartholdi the money he needed.

Nevertheless, Bartholdi and his supporters were not about to give up. They decided that France should pay for the statue. But the statue would have to rest on a giant platform, or **pedestal**. The Frenchmen hoped that the United States would pay for its pedestal and **foundation**.

Today, the statue stands on the star-shaped Fort Wood in the middle of Liberty Island. This island was once called Bedloe's Island.

A group called the Franco-American Union worked to raise money for the statue. They held dinners and dances in several French cities where people gave donations. Before long, there was enough money to begin work on the statue that would become more famous than anyone had ever dreamed.

While he was in the United States, Bartholdi also found a good location for the statue. It was a small island in New York Harbor called Bedloe's Island. He liked the location because people would see the statue as they entered the country by boat.

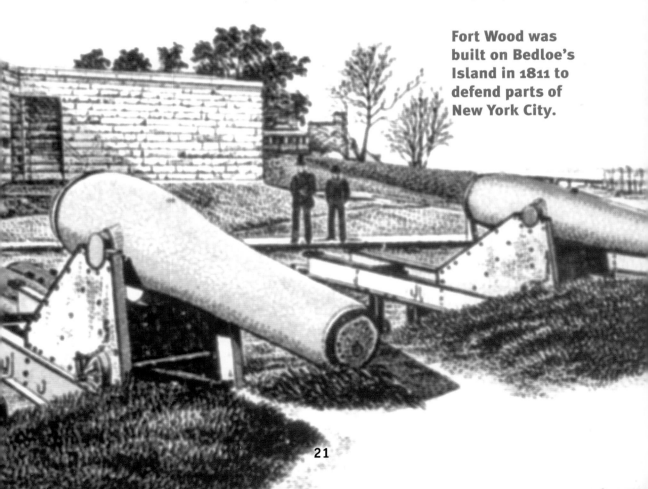

Fort Wood was built on Bedloe's Island in 1811 to defend parts of New York City.

Wooden molds were built first. Bartholdi shows a visitor a wooden mold of the statue's hand. Copper sheets were later hammered into the molds.

CHAPTER 4

Building the Statue

People could once climb a ladder from her shoulder to her torch!

Lady Liberty was to be much more than just a statue. She was also going to be a building. People would be able to walk into this statue. They could climb up 354 steps from the statue's feet to look out the windows in her crown.

Charlotte Bartholdi

Lady Liberty

Some people think that Bartholdi's mother was the model for Lady Liberty's face.

The giant statue would need to be light enough to be shipped across the ocean. It would need to be strong enough to withstand powerful winds out on its island. How could such a thing be built?

Bartholdi decided to make the statue out of a metal called copper. Copper is light and strong. The statue would be as brown and bright as a new penny when it arrived. But in time, the salty sea air would turn the copper blue-green.

Bartholdi created detailed drawings of the statue before he started to build models.

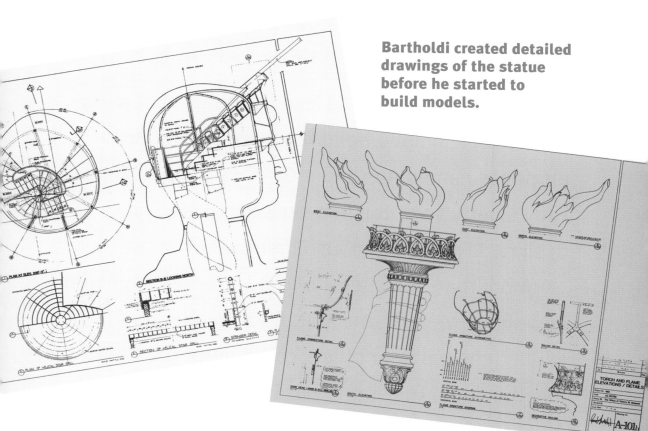

Hundreds of workers helped to build the statue piece by piece. You can see the statue's arm and hand in the background.

Bartholdi designed its face and shape, but many other people helped build the huge statue. An **engineer** named Alexandre Gustave Eiffel designed Lady Liberty's 120-ton iron skeleton. (Later, he designed France's famous Eiffel Tower.)

More than 300 sheets of copper were hammered into shape to make the statue's skin. Workers labeled the parts so others could piece them together later. The statue was like a giant puzzle!

Under the Statue

As the statue was being built, it became clear that it would need to rest on a strong pedestal. The well-known **architect** Richard Morris Hunt was hired to create the base for the statue. He designed an 89-foot (27 meter) **granite** pedestal.

Lady Liberty was going to be a massive statue. So the pedestal would need to sit on a strong, solid foundation. More than 27,000 tons of concrete would eventually be poured for the foundation. It would be the largest amount of concrete ever used for a single statue.

This diorama shows how workers may have smoothed out the bumps in Lady Liberty's face.

CHAPTER 5

Liberty on Display

Forty people can fit into the statue's head!

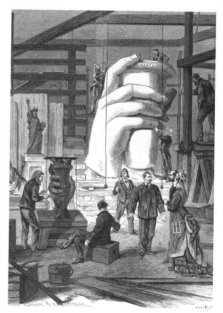

Workers rush to finish the statue's hand.

Unfortunately, Lady Liberty was not completed in time for the 100th birthday of the United States. Only her head, arm, and torch were finished by then. These parts were put on display to give people an exciting hint of what was to come.

Lady Liberty–
In Two Places at Once

The arm and torch traveled from France to the United States in 1876. They were displayed in Philadelphia, Pennsylvania, and New York City. People were amazed at the sight of such a huge sculpture. The arm and torch alone were 30 feet (9 meters) high. That's about as tall as five grown men standing one on top of the other.

Visitors could climb a ladder up the statue's arm and stand on a balcony outside her torch.

For the first time, Americans began to feel really excited about the statue. There was still not enough money to finish it, however.

People struggled to raise enough money to keep the project going. They even sold small copies of the Statue of Liberty. These proved to be popular. By the end of 1879, it finally looked as if there might be enough cash to complete the work.

In 1876, the statue's shiny head was put on display in Paris. Crowds loved it!

The statue's nose is 4 1/2 feet long!

Finally Finished

In June 1884, the Statue of Liberty was finished at last! Bartholdi was anxious to see it standing in New York Harbor. However, there was one major roadblock: the pedestal was far from completed. The Americans had run out of money.

Joseph Pulitzer ran a fund-raising ad in his newspaper in 1885.

A Paper Saves the Day

Joseph Pulitzer

Finally newspaper owner Joseph Pulitzer decided to help. In his paper, *The New York World*, he urged readers to give as much money as they could. Pulitzer stressed that Lady Liberty was a gift to all Americans. He promised to print the names of those who donated.

People throughout the country began to send money. Even children helped. Some gave their birthday money. School classes collected cash. By the summer of 1885, there was enough money.

Some children raised money for the pedestal by delivering newspapers.

Lady Liberty was carefully separated into 350 parts.

Meanwhile, workers in France were busy as well. They took the statue apart to send it to America. The parts were packed into 214 wooden crates. Some crates weighed as much as two cars!

On June 17, 1885, the French ship carrying the crates sailed into New York Harbor. Cheering crowds welcomed the statue to America.

It took more than a year to finish the pedestal and rebuild the statue. On October 28, 1886, the Statue of Liberty officially opened to the public. In New York City, more than 20,000 people marched in a parade that day in her honor. More than a million onlookers cheered the marchers. In a speech, President Grover Cleveland said, "We will not forget that Liberty has made here her home."

French people missed the statue, so they built a smaller one in Paris.

The Eiffel Tower

A statue worker examines cracks and holes in Liberty's foot.

CHAPTER 6

Liberty Lives On

Lady Liberty has seen a lot of changes since she was first put up. Time, weather, and even bombs have worn down the statue. People have fixed and even improved her, though. Today, the statue shines more brightly than ever before.

The statue was once used as a lighthouse, but its torch was not bright enough.

In 1916, during World War I, German agents set off a bomb on the coast of New Jersey, close to the Statue of Liberty. The statue's arm and torch were damaged. The arm was repaired, but it has been closed to visitors ever since.

Through the years, time and weather took an even bigger toll on Lady Liberty. In 1937, President Franklin Delano Roosevelt ordered major repairs. Water was seeping into her pedestal. So the

pedestal was covered with a giant sheet of copper. Workers also added heating, repaired the stairwells, and installed new elevators.

Her index finger is 8 feet long!

Workers had to take Lady Liberty's crown apart during repairs.

Liberty Stands Strong

By the 1980s, part of the statue's skeleton had worn away. Engineers added new steel bars. The statue also had a "bath" – its copper skin got a full cleaning. The torch was leaking, so a new torch was built. This one is covered in gold! These repairs took two years and cost $86 million.

Lady Liberty has been honored in many ways. In 1924, President Calvin Coolidge declared her to be a national monument. In 1960, Bedloe's Island was renamed Liberty Island.

The new torch no longer has lamps. It seems to glow by reflecting light from the sun.

The statue has fans of all ages from all across the world.

Today, thousands of visitors come to see Lady Liberty each year. They take a boat from Manhattan, in New York City, to Liberty Island. The inside of the statue has been closed since the terrorist attacks of September 11, 2001. However, visitors can tour Liberty Island, climb onto the pedestal to see the view, and visit the museum inside the pedestal. Maybe one day you will visit the Statue of Liberty, too.

Many films feature the Statue of Liberty. This scene is from the adventure movie from 2004 called *The Day After Tomorrow*.

Since she was built, Lady Liberty has inspired artists, musicians, poets, and filmmakers. In 1898, one of inventor Thomas Edison's first motion pictures was about the statue. Since then, Lady Liberty has appeared in more than 30 movies, including *Ghostbusters II* and *Batman*.

The Statue of Liberty had claimed a special spot in the hearts of many Americans. She still stands proudly in the harbor. She represents the struggle for liberty, in the past and in the present. ★

Year completed: 1886

Height including pedestal and foundation: 305 ft (93 m)

Length of hands: 16 ft 5 in (5 m)

Length of feet: 25 ft (7.6 m) (size 879 sandals)

Thickness of skin: .09 in (2.4 mm)

Weight of statue with pedestal: 51,725 tons

Weight of statue alone: 225 tons

Weight of fingernail: 3.5 lbs (1.6 kg)

Number of steps to the top: 354

Distance the statue sways in a storm: 3 in (8 cm)

Wind speed at which it sways 3 in: 50 miles (80 km) per hour

Did you find the truth?

F The Statue of Liberty used to be someone's house.

T The statue wears a size 879 shoe.

Resources

Books

Ashley, Susan. *The Statue of Liberty*.
  Milwaukee: Weekly Reader Early
  Learning, 2004.

Braithwaite, Jill. *The Statue of Liberty*.
  Minneapolis: Lerner Publications, 2003.

Curlee, Lynn. *Liberty*. New York:
  Atheneum Books for Young Readers, 2000.

De Capua, Sarah. *How People Immigrate*.
  Danbury, CT: Children's Press, 2004.

Firestone, Mary. *The Statue of Liberty*.
  Minneapolis: Picture Window Books, 2006.

Fontes, Justine, and Ron Fontes. *France*.
  Danbury, CT: Children's Press, 2003.

Jango-Cohen, Judith. *Ellis Island*.
  Danbury, CT: Children's Press, 2005.

Murray, Julie. *Statue of Liberty*.
  Edina, MN: Abdo, 2003.

Rau, Dana Meachen. *The Statue of Liberty*.
  Minneapolis: Compass Point Books, 2002.

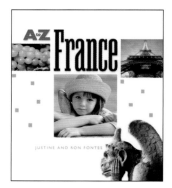

Organizations and Web Sites

Ben's Guide to U.S. Government for Kids —
Statues and Memorials
http://bensguide.gpo.gov/3-5/symbols/ladyliberty.html
See this Web site for more information on the Statue of Liberty.

The Statue of Liberty
www.nps.gov/stli
Visit this Web site for lots of information about
Lady Liberty's history.

Welcome to the Statue of Liberty —
Ellis Island Foundation, Inc.
www.statueofliberty.org
Check out this Web site for some fun facts about the statue.

Places to Visit

Ellis Island
Immigration Museum
Ellis Island Statue of Liberty
National Monument
New York, NY 10004
212-344-0996
www.ellisisland.com

Statue of Liberty
National Park Service
Statue of Liberty
National Monument
Liberty Island
New York, NY 10004
212-363-3200
www.nps.gov/stli

Important Words

architect–(ar-kuh-tekt) a person who designs buildings and directs their construction

citizens–people who who live with full right and protections in a particular country

continents–the seven major bodies of land on Earth

emperor–a leader who holds all the power over a country or a group of countries

engineer–a person who uses scientific knowledge and rules to design and build things such as bridges and tunnels

foundation–the solid structure on which a building or statue rests

granite–a hard, gray stone used in building

liberty–freedom from the control of others

pedestal–the base for a statue

Revolutionary War–a war from 1775 to 1783 that gave the 13 American colonies independence from Great Britain, forming the United States of America

sculptor–someone who carves or shapes items out of stone, wood, or metal

symbol–(sim-bul) an object that stands for something else

Index

Page numbers in **bold** indicate illustrations

About the Author

Award-winning author Elaine Landau has a bachelor's degree from New York University and a master's degree in Library and Information Science. She has written more than 300 nonfiction books for children and young adults.

The Statue of Liberty is very special to Ms. Landau. It was the first thing her father saw when he came to America many years ago. Ms. Landau has visited Lady Liberty many times herself. She likes it better each time she sees it!

Elaine Landau lives in Miami, Florida, with her husband and son. You can visit her at her Web site www.elainelandau.com.

PHOTOGRAPHS © 2008: age fotostock: 16, 17 (Kord.com), 37 (Rafael Macia/allphoto); Alamy Images/Dennis Hallinan: 11; Corbis Images: 40 (Ed Bailey/Bettmann), 6, 8, 14 left, 32 right, 33, 38 (Bettmann), 39 (Hulton-Deutsch Collection), 5 top (George F. Ireland), back cover, 35 (Bob Krist), 9 (Edwin Levick/The Mariners' Museum), 3, 43 (Robert Llewellyn), 15 right (Museum of the City of New York), 4 top (Tetra Images), 22; Doug Smith: 5 bottom; Everett Collection, Inc.: 42; Getty Images: 15 left (Felix Francois Barthelemy), 7 (CSA Plastock), 20 (Hulton Archive), 13 left, 13 right (Thomas Northcut), 41 (Erin Patrice O'Brien), 10 (PhotoLink), 28 (Roger Viollet/Branger); JupiterImages/Alan Schein: cover; Library of Congress: 26, 27, 31, 34; National Archives and Records Administration: 19; Scholastic Library Publishing, Inc.: 44 bottom, 44 center, 44 top; ShutterStock, Inc./Tom Nance: 18; Statue of Liberty National Monument/National Park Service: 4 center, 14 right, 23, 32 left (American Museum of Immigration), 30 (Library of Philadelphia), 25 right, 25 left (Swanke Hayden Connell Ltd.), 4 bottom, 12, 21, 24 left, 36; Superstock, Inc.: 29; TIPS Images/Kathleen Campbel/Stone: 24 right.